Easy Rambles

In The
Langdale Valleys

Vivienne Crow

Questa

ISBN 978-1-898808-36-7

Maps:
The maps accompanying the walks in this book are purely
diagrammatic, and are based on maps produced by Harvey Maps
(Licence No. 86413/3 © Harvey Map Services Ltd.)

Published by
Questa Publishing Limited

www.questapublishing.co.uk

CONTENTS

NOTE

No attempt has been made to grade the walks in this book, as this is too subjective. Use the information about distance and height gain to calculate how long the walk will take.

INTRODUCTION

The two gorgeous valleys that make up the Langdales are at the rocky heart of the Lake District, home to that most iconic of British mountain images, the Langdale Pikes. If you enjoy walking, you've come to the right place! With dozens of paths and tracks going off in all directions, there is plenty to keep ramblers of all abilities entertained for weeks, if not months. Whether you're following valley paths or heading on to the gentler, low-lying fells – both of which are covered in this book – you'll constantly be surrounded by some of the most magnificent mountain scenery that this country has to offer. Crags and rocky ridges dot the skyline while tarns glitter like jewels in breathtaking passes or lurk, cold and dark, in mountain cirques. Waterfalls plunge through deep, forbidding chasms. And, all along the valley floor, ancient drystone walls carve up the farmland before snaking up into the hills.

As you first head west from Ambleside, on either side of the River Brathay you encounter rolling, wooded slopes that hide pretty tarns and the occasional rocky knoll thrusting up through the surrounding grass and bracken to hint at things to come further upstream. Here, walkers can head up to secluded Lily Tarn (see walk five) or climb on to the diminutive Black Crag, which has some surprisingly good views for such a little fell (see walk nine). Beautiful Loughrigg Tarn, with the Langdale Pikes forming the perfect backdrop for photographers intent on capturing picture postcard scenes, can be easily reached on foot from Skelwith Bridge (see Walk 1).

The A593 crosses the River Brathay at Skelwith Bridge, heading for Coniston. It is here that visitors turn off, along the B5343, for Great Langdale. The first village you reach is Elterwater, just west of the reedy lake with which it shares a name. The village developed as an industrial settlement based on quarrying and the manufacture of gunpowder. Little remains of the latter, but there is plenty of evidence of the slate quarries throughout both Great and Little Langdale.

A peaceful stroll from Elterwater along becks and through pretty woodland takes you past two lovely waterfalls and pays a visit to the less visited valley of Little Langdale (see walk six). Heading north on to Dow Bank and across the top of the Megs Gill waterfalls, ramblers get a chance to stride out along a low, grassy ridge with spectacular views towards the head of the valley and to visit some prehistoric rock art (see walk eight). For the slightly more adventurous, Lingmoor Fell and Side Pike can also be explored (see Walk 10).

Continuing deeper into Great Langdale, Chapel Stile is the valley's main village. The picturesque Holy Trinity church was built in 1857 of green slate from the nearby quarry. Several of the walks drop in on Chapel Stile, including route three, which follows Great Langdale Beck as it passes beneath the Langdale Pikes. Beyond Chapel Stile there is little in the way of settlement – just a handful of farms and the hotels – until the road's westward progression is halted by the high wall of rock thrown up by the ridge comprising Crinkle Crags and Bow Fell. Route two takes walkers right up to the very base of these mighty mountains – with only 138m of ascent, there couldn't be an easier way to see this amazing scenery and wonder at the natural forces that initially moulded and then shaped this landscape. Volcanic activity, sedimentary processes and glaciations all played their part. Essentially, the Lake District is a massive volcanic dome fissured by tectonic forces and then sculpted by huge rivers of ice to create a spray of valleys and dividing mountain ranges radiating from a central hub like spokes from a wheel.

The B5343 ends at the Old Dungeon Ghyll Hotel close to the head of the valley, but a narrow road winds its way steeply uphill from here – to Blea Tarn. Like Loughrigg Tarn, this small but perfectly formed body of water is a great place from which to view the Langdale Pikes. From here, walk seven heads along the base of Lingmoor Fell and down into Little Langdale, visiting the site where the area's Norse settlers used to hold important meetings. Little Langdale is also visited on route four, which explores the fascinating quarried landscape to the south of the valley. Even those who find industrial archaeology a total bore can't fail to be impressed by some of the sights on this walk.

Despite man's far-reaching effects on the landscape, the Lake District remains relatively rich in wildlife. High fell fauna include foxes, hares and stoats. Herds of red deer can sometimes be seen above the treeline, while the woods are home to badgers, roe deer, voles, shrews, occasional otters and the iconic red squirrel, sadly under threat from the incursion of the more dominant American greys into one of their last bastions in England. There have even been sightings in recent years of pine martens, one of the rarest and most elusive of British mammals.

The birds that make the fell-tops their home all year round include ravens, buzzards and peregrines. Lower down, in the spring, you'll encounter migratory species such as redstart, pied flycatcher, wood warbler and tree pipit as well as the year-round residents, including chaffinch, green and great-spotted woodpeckers, nuthatch and sparrowhawk. While you might catch sight of waterfowl on the tarns, the rivers and becks are home to dippers, wagtails and common sandpipers.

Depending on the time of year, it is possible to see any of these birds and mammals on the walks in this book, especially if you are up with the dawn or walking late in the evening.

1

LOUGHRIGG TARN

A short, easy walk that uses mostly a combination of quiet lanes and pleasant tracks to visit one of the most beautifully situated low-level tarns in the Lake District – Loughrigg Tarn. You'll be stopped in your tracks by your first glimpse of it, but it won't be the grassy slopes leading down to the water's edge or the pretty cottages and woods that command your attention; it will be the backdrop provided by the Langdale Pikes that will be sure to hypnotise you. Watch out for the rare downy emerald dragonfly near the tarn and red squirrels and roe deer in the woods.

> **Start/Finish**: Roadside parking on the B5343
> near the Skelwith Bridge Hotel (NY344034)
> **Distance**: 4km (2½ miles)
> **Height gain**: 136m (447ft)

1. From the junction of the B5343 Langdale road and the A593 in Skelwith Bridge take the narrow, restricted-access lane heading uphill (NNE) to the right of a row of white cottages. This is on the opposite side of the B5343 to the Talbot Bar of the Skelwith Bridge Hotel. Turn right at a T-junction, quickly crossing a tiny beck. Almost immediately, turn left along a surfaced track and then swing right at Tarn Foot Farm, as indicated by the waymarkers. Turn left at a crossing of paths to go through a gate to the immediate right of Tarn Foot Lodge. This track soon leads to the railings above Loughrigg Tarn and that first, magnificent view.

> *Loughrigg Tarn, which sits at an altitude of 320ft, has been a popular spot for centuries. Wordsworth described it as a "most beautiful example" and gave it its nickname*

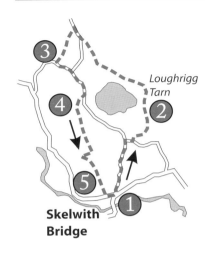

Loughrigg
Tarn

Skelwith
Bridge

"Diana's looking glass" after the Italian Lake Nemi, said to be the mirror of Diana, who was the Roman warrior goddess of nature and fertility.

If you are here during the early summer, you may be lucky enough to catch a glimpse of the downy emerald dragonfly near the tarn. The dragonfly is generally only found in south-east England, but there are a few colonies in the Lake District. It isn't easy to identify because it rarely rests in accessible places, so the best way to identify it is in flight. It is medium-sized, bronze-coloured and has bright green eyes. Males patrol in a low, fast flight, pausing to hover at intervals.

2. There is a permissive path that goes around the tarn itself, but you get a better feel for the lovely setting by maintaining some height. Continue along the pleasant, tree-lined track that skirts the eastern side of this popular beauty-spot and passes some lovely cottages. When you reach a road, turn right. As you draw level with some cottages on the right, turn left through a gate with a fingerpost beside it. The path on the ground is not clear now; aim for a small gate where a wall meets a fence in the SW corner of the field. Beyond this, continue in the same direction, with a wall to your left for the first 80 meters or so. You then go through a gap in this wall and walk with it on your immediate right.

3. Cross the awkward stile hidden in the bottom corner of the field and turn left along the quiet road. At the next road junction, turn right.

4. About 350 metres beyond this junction, having passed a footpath coming up from the tarn, turn right along a track. This eventually becomes a narrow path and enters the private grounds of Neaum Crag via a small gate. An asphalt lane heads down between wooden cabins. Keep your eyes peeled for the waymarkers through this shady site – you head straight down the hill at first and then, after a bend to the right, you reach a junction. Go straight across here and then swing slightly right. You soon find yourself walking downhill on a narrower path between wooden railings. This turns sharp left after going through a gate – and you now have metal railings on your right and a drystone wall on your left.

5. Beyond the next gate, you are back out in the open again. Head straight down the grassy slope towards a wall corner, always aiming for the hotel. Once through the kissing-gate, you are back out on the B5343.

2

INTO MICKLEDEN

With some of the Lake District's most iconic mountains towering above you, this walk takes you almost to the head of Langdale. As you stroll along valley paths, you get just a teasing taste of this magnificent walking country and get to see some of the hill farms that have helped to shape it. A wide beck has to be forded about half-way through the walk, but this shouldn't present any difficulties except after heavy rain.

> **Start/Finish**: The National Trust pay and display car park in Great Langdale (NY294064)
> **Distance**: 6.6km (4 miles)
> **Height gain**: 138m (452ft)

1. Leave the car park via the vehicle entrance and turn left along the road. In about 30 metres, turn right along a farm track, signposted Oak Howe. Go through the gate to the left of the buildings at Side House and then cross the plank bridge. Bear right to follow a small beck upstream for about 50 metres and then cross the bridge and ladder stile over the wall on your right.

2. A narrow but clear path contours the hillside and leads to a second ladder stile. Beyond this, cross the remains of an old wall. Soon after this, bear left along a less obvious path heading slightly uphill. The route on the ground is unclear, but you should try to walk parallel with the fence about 200 metres up the hill to your left. Before long, you pick up the line of a fence on your right and go through a kissing-gate. Continue alongside the fence until you reach a wall.

3. Go through the kissing-gate on your right and descend through

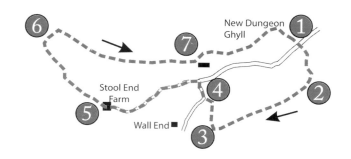

the trees. After the next kissing-gate, swing half-right down the grassy slope to pass through a gap in a wall followed by two gates in quick succession to enter the National Trust campsite. Continue in the same direction, making for a wall corner and then walk with the wall on your left. Turn left along the track and leave the campsite via a gate.

4. Turn right along the road and, at a sharp right-hand bend, turn left along a surfaced farm track. You are now looking straight up towards the head of Oxendale backed by the impressive buttresses of Crinkle Crags. The track leads right up to Stool End Farm where you need to keep a close eye on the signposts guiding you between the farm buildings. Basically, the right of way swings right and then left, climbing to a gate to leave the farmyard.

5. Beyond the gate, turn right to walk with a wall on your right. Ahead of you is the valley of Mickleden with Rossett Pike and Rossett Gill at its head. Soon after a kissing-gate, the path swings slightly right to pass between two walls. When the wall on your right swings away, keep straight ahead for a few more metres, but then, when the main track swings left, bear right along a narrower path that soon runs parallel with the beck.

On the other side of the beck are the steep, scree-covered slopes of Pike O'Stickle. These are home to one of

12

Cumbria's most fascinating Neolithic sites – the Langdale stone axe factory. High up on this mountainside, Neolithic workers would have quarried the exposed seam of 'greenstone', a flint-like volcanic rock, and roughed out axe heads from it. It is assumed the heads were then taken to the coast for sharpening and polishing. There was a significant trade in these tools and Langdale axes have been found as far away as Cornwall. The site of the axe factory is on horribly steep and unstable ground and a visit is most definitely not recommended.

6. You now need to ford the beck. Just upstream of the abutments of the old bridge is a weir. As long as you aren't attempting this walk after heavy rain, you can easily cross the top of this, but be careful because the submerged stones are slippery. Once across, make straight towards the steep slopes ahead. In about 120 metres, you reach a track, along which you turn right. After 1.4km, you will see the buildings of Middle Fell Farm to the right. Don't be tempted by the track down to the farm; instead, continue with the wall on your right until you reach a small gate in it. Now bear half-left (not sharp left) to climb to a kissing-gate that is tucked just out of sight at the moment.

The popular Old Dungeon Ghyll Hotel is just below the path here. It originally played a dual role as both a farm and an inn, and was known as Middlefell Inn at the end of the 19th century. These were the days of horse-drawn coaches bringing visitors from Little Langdale over Blea Tarn Pass. They would stop at the top and blow their horn, a signal to get lunch or tea ready - the number of blasts informed the staff of the number of passengers requiring a meal.

The wealthy historian Professor G M Trevelyan bought the hotel in the early 1900s for £4,100. He gifted it, and 50 acres of adjoining land, to the National Trust in 1929 – the organisation's first property in Langdale. Later, he also bought Stool End Farm, Wall End Farm, Mill Beck Farm and Harry Place Farm, all of which were eventually donated to the Trust.

7. You are now on a rough path with a wall on your right. Soon after crossing a beck via a bridge, the path climbs to a kissing-gate. Just after this, go through the gate on your right and follow the muddy path steeply down into the National Trust car park.

THE NATIONAL TRUST

The origins of the National Trust, one of the largest conservation charities in Europe, are rooted deeply in the Lake District. In 1875, Canon Hardwicke Rawnsley, vicar of Low Wray Church near Hawkshead, and later Crosthwaite in Keswick, met the social reformer Octavia Hill. Together with lawyer Sir Robert Hunter, they crusaded passionately for a National Trust to be formed to buy and preserve places of natural beauty and historic interest for the nation.

The first building purchased by the trust was Alfriston Clergy House in Sussex, bought for £10 in 1896, but it was in 1902, when the 108-acre Brandelhow estate on the shores of Derwentwater came on the market that the trust set about its most ambitious scheme to date. A brilliant and inspirational speaker, Rawnsley led the campaign to raise funds for the purchase and received nationwide support. The scheme's success was never in doubt with him at the helm, and Princess Louise, daughter of Queen Victoria and a supporter of the National Trust's work, performed Brandelhow's opening ceremony on October 6, 1902.

Today, the charity protects a massive 123,500 acres of land in the Lake District – that's about a quarter of the total area covered by the National Park.

3

GREAT LANGDALE BECK

Few Lakeland valley routes pass through such magnificent surroundings as this one. Starting from Elterwater and with the majestic Langdale Pikes dominating the view for much of the time, it makes its way up into Great Langdale using a combination of lanes, tracks and paths. It then heads back along the valley bottom, dropping in on the pretty village of Chapel Stile on the way.

> **Start/Finish**: The National Trust pay and display car park in Elterwater (NY327047)
> **Distance**: 9.7km (6 miles)
> **Height gain**: 190m (622ft)

1. Turn left out of the car park and cross Great Langdale Beck. Walk along the road for about 300 metres and then, soon after passing the driveway of the Eltermere Inn on your left, turn right up a narrow lane – signposted Coniston. At a fork, bear right.

> *Elterwater developed as an industrial settlement based on quarrying and the manufacture of gunpowder. The gunpowder works were built beside the fast-flowing beck – on the site of what is now the Langdale Estate country club – by Kendal man David Huddlestone in 1824. To ensure a constant and reliable water supply, Stickle Tarn, high above the valley, was dammed. Charcoal was supplied by the local alder coppices, while sulphur and saltpetre were imported from abroad.*
>
> *By the start of the 20th century, the gunpowder works*

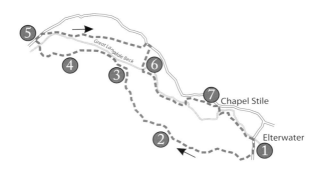

employed about 80 people, known locally as 'Powder Monkeys'. Many men died in explosions there, one of the earliest of which killed five people in 1840. The works were finally closed in 1928.

2. Eventually, you emerge from the trees into glorious Great Langdale, soon passing the farm at Baysbrown. Keep to the left of the buildings. A little way beyond the farm, bear left at a fork, climbing gently to a second fork, where you bear right. A rather conspicuous signpost indicates this is the way to Great Langdale and Dungeon Ghyll. As you approach a stone barn near the valley bottom at Oak Howe, make sure you swing right at a waymarked fork.

3. When you reach the barn, turn left – signposted New Dungeon Ghyll. Keep to the waymarked path, which swings sharp left to pass between two dilapidated walls.

The Langdale Pikes appear for the first time ahead of you now. Before long, the pyramid-like top of Bow Fell can be seen, and then Crinkle Crags comes into view too. Now you are truly among Lake District giants.

4. The path climbs to ford a beck and then goes through a gap in a

wall before descending towards Side House. Just before you reach the buildings, cross the wooden bridge on your right and go through the kissing-gate. The track swings right and makes its way to the main valley road.

Side House has a strong connection with the wealthy historian Professor G M Trevelyan, who gave many Langdale properties to the National Trust. It was bought in 1963, the year after his death, with money provided by his daughter and his old Cambridge college, Trinity.

5. Turn right and, in about 70 metres, turn right into the Lake District National Park car park. Keep close to the wall on your right and you will soon find yourself walking along a rough track in the valley bottom. Turn right when you reach the road and, in another 90 metres, go through a gate on your right – signposted Baysbrown. After walking along the track for about 350 metres, do not be tempted by a route swinging round to the right.

6. Immediately after crossing the gated bridge over Great Langdale Beck, turn left along a track heading downstream. It eventually crosses a humpback bridge and swings right. When it then swings left near the road, leave it by turning right along a path. As you reach the buildings, follow the sealed road to the left. Then, making sure you don't head up to the farm buildings, turn right at the next track junction to walk with the school's wall on your left. Keep the wall on your left until you drop to the road.

7. Turn right and, soon after passing the Wainwright's Inn, turn right again to cross Great Langdale Beck via a footbridge. Once on the other side, turn left. Eventually, you reach a minor road along which you bear left. Turn left at the T-junction to return to the car park.

4

LITTLE LANGDALE AND THE SLATE QUARRIES

Walkers have a chance to explore some of the fascinating remains of the slate quarrying industry on this stroll through the lovely countryside just south of Little Langdale. Even if you have no interest in industrial archaeology, you can't fail to be impressed by the deep, sheer-sided pits, the blue-green pools and the spectacular caverns you will see on this walk.

The route follows clear, mostly surfaced tracks through pleasant woodland and along the side of open fells. It also visits Little Langdale – home to the Three Shires Inn – about two-thirds of the way through. If you set off in the late morning, you'll be just in time for a lunchtime drink.

> **Start/Finish**: Quarry at Hodge Close (NY316017)
> **Distance**: 6km (4 miles)
> **Height gain**: 247m (810ft)

1. Begin by heading back along the road on which you entered the quarry, but only for a short while. Just before the road leaves the quarry proper, strike off to the left and pass to the right of a very deep and steep-sided quarry pit. There is no path on the ground here, but you soon reach a gate. Go through it to access National Trust land at Holme Fell and turn right along the woodland track. This heads gently uphill for more than 1km.

You can't fail to notice evidence of quarrying all over the fellsides in this area. The slate has been worked

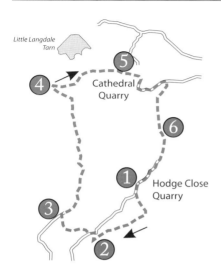

Little Langdale Tarn

Cathedral Quarry

Hodge Close Quarry

since Roman times, although historians know little about the industry before the end of the 17th century. Despite fierce competition from Welsh slate, great expansion took place in the early part of the 19th century, and the industry received a massive boost when, in 1859, the railway reached nearby Coniston. Sadly though, this was short-lived – and the industry's decline began in the 1880s.

World War One, in particular, caused huge problems for quarries such as Hodge Close. With the skilled men away at war, the steep walls became unstable and rock falls started to occur, damaging equipment. Eventually, the pumps were stopped and water began to fill the pits. Quarrying restarted when the men returned, but then World War Two began and the pits deteriorated again. Hodge Close was finally closed in the 1950s.

2. When the track starts descending, you will see a farmhouse on the road below. You pass above the farm and drop to a wall. Now turn sharp right, and follow the grassy track to the farm. Turn left at the road. Immediately after the buildings, turn right to go through

a wooden farm gate – signposted High Tilberthwaite. You walk alongside the wall on your right for 20 metres and then swing left, making for a small, fenced area of trees. At the fence corner, turn right to go through a squeeze stile. Turn left immediately, trying not to lose height, and then cross a stile in a fence. Follow the trail through the trees and drop to a clearer path, along which you turn right. Go through the gate and make for High Tilberthwaite Farm.

3. Turn right at the farm road. Ignore the bridleway that bears right past the farm buildings; instead, head for the track going uphill beside a low building to your left. This wide, stony track climbs slowly. Then, when it starts descending, you see Lingmoor Fell straight ahead of you and the Langdales peeping over its NW shoulder.

4. Turn right at a junction with another clear track. The track passes one cottage on your left and then drops down to some more buildings. About 250 metres after these buildings, having passed a gate in the wall on your left leading to Slater Bridge, the track goes through a large gate. About 120 metres beyond this gate, you will see a gated track on your right. Although the main route continues along the track, this gate provides you with an opportunity to explore the disused quarry workings here.

> Although the gate is locked, there is a stile beside it. The track climbs to a short tunnel that leads to the impressive cavern known as Cathedral Quarry with 13m-high walls. It is also possible to explore other, longer tunnels and old workings from here, but please bear in mind that you will need a torch and there are dangers associated with these old quarries, including very low ceilings and the potential for rock falls.

> Although this quarry has not been worked for some time, there are still a few sites that continue to produce Lakeland slate, famous for its durability and its colours. Each of the quarries and mines still operating produces

its own unique slate – sea green or silvery green from Kirkstone, dark blues from Brathay, the famous green slate of Honister, and the black and green products from the quarries around Coniston. More than 85 per cent of the slate is unsuitable for the traditional market – roofing slates – so there has been a lot of diversification in recent years, and the quarries now produce slate for floor tiles, kitchen worktops, fireplaces and garden water features.

5. Back on the main route, continue along the track until you see a gated, wooden footbridge on your left. The track now swings right. As soon as it does so, turn left along a narrow beckside trail through the trees. This comes out on to a surfaced lane, along which you turn left. The lane bends sharp right near the buildings at Stang End. As it then swings back to the left, turn right along a rough track – signposted Hodge Close and Coniston.

6. After going through a few gates, the track swings right, through the woods. Keep to the surfaced lane when you reach the cottages at Hodge Close. This soon returns you to your starting point, passing to the right of the huge pit you passed at the beginning of the walk.

Be very careful if you decide to explore this area – with little warning, you can find yourself on unstable ground at the top of a steep drop. This is no place for small children or uncontrolled dogs.

This massive excavation has resulted in sheer sides that are popular with abseilers. Divers too find plenty of interest here – the quarry pool has a maximum depth of about 100ft and there is an underwater tunnel entrance that leads to three chambers and two interconnecting tunnels.

5

ABOVE THE RIVER BRATHAY

This walk starts with a steep climb from Clappersgate, but don't let that put you off – after just 800 metres, all the hard work is over and you're left with nothing but sheer enjoyment. Your first stop is lovely Lily Tarn, and then you make your meandering way across this low moorland towards Loughrigg Fell and a delightful path close to its base. Quiet lanes drop you down to Skelwith Bridge and some more country roads then lead up to Skelwith Fold, from where you get a superb view of the Langdale Pikes. A good track, farm paths and some road walking then return you to the parking area.

> **Start/Finish**: Parking area near Clappersgate, beside the River Brathay (NY365033). If you are coming from Ambleside, turn left towards Hawkshead when you reach Clappersgate. The parking area is on the right a few hundred metres beyond the junction.
> **Distance**: 8km (5 miles)
> **Height gain**: 274m (900ft)

1. From the parking area, walk back along the minor road towards Clappersgate – with the river on your left. At the junction with the A593, carefully cross straight over and head up the narrow path slightly to the right. After going through a gate, a reasonably clear path continues straight ahead, hugging the side of the steep slope and providing good views of the surrounding countryside.

2. When you reach a wall, don't go through the gap in it; instead, turn sharp right to climb more steeply. At the top of this initial climb, bear right to keep to the right of the wall. Turn left at a massive, sprawling cairn at the base of a rocky knoll. You quickly reach another path,

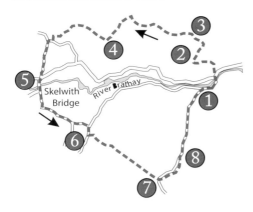

along which you swing right (NNE) and then a junction of several paths, where you turn left (NNW). Having passed to the left of a shallow pool, you climb slightly and then drop to the side of Lily Tarn, identifiable from the small tree growing in the middle of it.

3. Keep to the S edge of the water, quickly crossing the outlet stream. The path heads mostly W now – in the general direction of Crinkle Crags in the distance. Keep to the clearest path at all times, following the line of the wall which is a little way over to the left at first. As you regain the wall, the path swings more NW and drops down to and through a kissing-gate. Don't be tempted by any paths up to the right on to the higher ground – keep following the line of the wall until you reach a small beck. Ford this, climb the slope on the other side and then turn left along the clear path at the base of Loughrigg.

You soon find yourself walking with a drystone wall over to your left. Walls like this are an integral part of the Cumbrian landscape – creating the small enclosures that are so typical of Lakeland valleys, and running for seemingly endless miles on the open fell-tops. Built without mortar or cement, some of them date back to the late 13th century when the Cistercian monks of Furness Abbey farmed much of the region, but most were built during the Enclosure movement of the 18th and 19th centuries.

The walls are built on a foundation of two parallel rows of large boulders on either side of a trench. The sides are then built up and the inside is filled with smaller stones. At regular intervals, a layer of 'throughstones' is placed across the entire width of the wall to strengthen it. Walls tend to be wider at the bottom than at the top – for stability. They are generally topped with a row of slanting or vertical stones, known as 'cam-stones', to discourage sheep from climbing over the wall.

4. When the path splits, take the left branch down to a large gate. Don't go through this; instead, stick with the level path around the base of the fell with magnificent views ahead of the Langdale Pikes. Go through a gate and head downhill on the loose, stony track until you reach a junction of lanes at Tarn Foot Lodge. Continue straight across and then bear left near the farm. Turn right along the minor road and then take the next road turning on your left.

5. When you reach the main road junction in Skelwith Bridge, carefully cross the B5343 and then head along the A593 in the direction of Coniston, passing the Skelwith Bridge Hotel on your right. Just after the bridge, the road swings right. Take the minor road to the left of the bend – towards the community centre. Bear left at the next fork – towards Skelwith Fold and Brathay.

When you reach the first of the buildings on the hill, pause a while; slowly turn round and prepare for an amazing sight. The magnificent Langdale Pikes dominate the scene straight ahead, and Pike O'Blisco and Crinkle Crags look pretty impressive too. Just imagine what it must be like to live in the house up to the left and wake to that view from your conservatory every morning!

6. Turn right at the next road junction – signposted Hawkshead. When you see the postbox, turn left along the sealed track, towards Pull Wyke. Turn right at the gates of the caravan park. Passing through

several gates along the way, you are on a good track for about 700 metres until you reach the end of the wall on your right. Now keep to the left of the tiny beck. Soon after the metal kissing-gate, the path fades to nothing. Keep heading SE to drop towards some buildings. Go through the small gate at the bottom of this grassy slope, turn left along the farm track and then cross straight over the road to go through the gap in the wall opposite.

7. Turn left along the roadside path. This soon climbs some steps and you have to walk along the road for a short while. Then, when you reach a turning on your right, you regain the roadside path – in the trees to the right of the asphalt. This again drops to the road at a bus stop opposite the entrance to the Skelwith Fold Caravan Park.

8. There used to be a permissive path through the woods on the other side of the road that would take you back to the parking area. At the time of writing, this had been closed, but the National Park was consulting with the landowner about reopening it. If it is still closed, simply turn right and follow the road back to the starting point.

Brathay Hall, close to the parking area, is home to the Brathay Trust, a national charity that helps vulnerable and disadvantaged children and young people to realise their potential.

6

ELTERWATER AND THE WATERFALLS

Starting with a peaceful stroll beside Great Langdale Beck and Elter Water, this fairly gentle walk takes in two relatively little-visited Lake District waterfalls – Skelwith Force and Colwith Force. Using mostly well-signposted and clear tracks, it then meanders through pretty woodland into Little Langdale for some gorgeous views across the tarn to the surrounding fells. The route back to Elterwater offers more tantalising glimpses of the distant mountains.

> **Start/Finish**: National Trust pay and display car park in Elterwater (NY327047)
> **Distance**: 8.9km (5½ miles)
> **Height gain**: 256m (840ft)

1. Before you've even left the car park, walk over to the wall beside the beck and then turn left, soon going through a gate to access a constructed riverside path. Ignore a turning to the left in the woods and you will emerge close to the water's edge again. Continue alongside the beck and go through a gate to reach a bridge. You will cross this bridge in a short while, but, for now, keep to the beckside path for a view of Skelwith Force in about 80 metres.

> *This waterfall may only be about five metres high, but it's in a pretty woodland setting and can look impressive after heavy rain as the beck forces it way through the rocks.*

2. Retrace your steps to cross the bridge, and then continue along the clear path. Soon after passing a house on your left, you join another path coming in from the left. You leave the woods via a kissing-gate

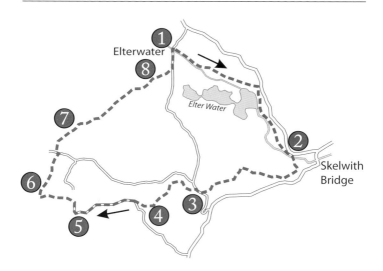

and, a little later, join a rough track coming in from the left. After passing in front of Park House, head to the left of a tiny shed to pass through two metal kissing-gates in quick succession. The path leads up to Elterwater Park guesthouse. Swing left as you cross the yard to reach the access road. Cross diagonally to your right to pick up the continuation of the footpath. The clear path crosses some stiles to reach another private road. Cross straight over and go through the gate to head downhill. After a couple more stiles and a short section of riverside walking, you reach a minor road along which you turn right.

3. Walk along the asphalt for about 80 metres and then turn left to cross a stile in a wall, immediately followed by a stile in a fence – signposted High Park. The path swings right and you have to clamber over some slippery rocks to gain a riverside path. Turn right at a T-junction. To get a good view of Colwith Force, bear right when you reach a fork in the path at the bottom of some stone steps. Once you've seen the

13-metre high waterfall, retrace your steps to the fork and then bear right to climb the steps. With a steep drop on your right, the path swings round for another view of the falls and then splits. Bear left, soon climbing gradually through the woods.

4. At a junction with another path near the edge of the woods, bear right, through a kissing-gate. Follow the wall on your right for a few metres and then follow the path through the gate. When you reach High Park, go through the gate. Turn right towards the farm and then swing left through the yard. Go through the large wooden gate on your left, opposite the barn, and then turn right along the surfaced lane. On reaching the next set of buildings at Stang End, bear right – signposted Elterwater and Ambleside.

5. The lane crosses a small beck after which it becomes rougher underfoot. It then joins a track coming in from the left to drop to a beck near a footbridge. Continue with the beck on your right, passing the entrance to some disused quarries on your left (see Walk 4). Go through a kissing-gate in the wall on your right and then cross Slater Bridge.

> *This ancient bridge is thought to have provided workers with access to the slate quarries, hence its name. There are also suggestions that the bridge may even date back to Roman times or that it was named after the Sleyther family in the late 14th century.*

6. Once on the other side of the beck, ignore the path off to the right. Climb gently with a wall on your right. When you reach some farm buildings, bear left on to a track that takes you to the road. Turn left and then immediately right on to a surfaced lane – signposted Ambleside.

7. As you pass a farm, the going underfoot becomes increasingly rough. Keep to this track, ignoring any paths off to the left, for more than 1km (about ½ mile).

8. On reaching a surfaced lane, keep straight on and then turn left at the road. The car park is now about 300 metres ahead.

The name Elter Water is said to come from the Norse for 'Swan Lake' and whooper swans from Scandinavia do sometimes grace the lake during the winter.

Norse words crop up all over the map of Cumbria. It is generally believed that the first Vikings came into the area some time before the second half of the ninth century. These weren't the raping, pillaging Danish raiders of modern mythology, but settlers who had come from Norway via Ireland and the Isle of Man. While the Anglo-Saxon settlers farmed the valleys around the mountain fringes, these pastoralist Norsemen began making their homes in the uplands – and leaving their legacy on our maps and in the local dialect. If you look at a modern map of Norway you will quickly discover why the Cumbrians call their hills and mountains fells; 'fjell' means mountain in Norwegian. The word for waterfall is 'foss', which becomes 'force' in the Lake District; 'tjorn' becomes tarn; and 'bekkr' beck.

7

LITTLE LANGDALE AND BLEA TARN

Taking a walk through Little Langdale is a little like taking a step back in time. With only one narrow road running through the valley, there is relatively little traffic; the architecture is of a distinctly vernacular type, some of it owned and protected for posterity by the National Trust; and there is evidence all around of past industries and previous settlers.
This varied route gives you the chance to experience this lovely valley from a combination of farm paths, valley tracks and a lovely trail along the base of Lingmoor Fell. It passes the impressive remains of Cathedral Quarry, Slater Bridge and a Norse ting mound.
Saving the best until last, it ends at Blea Tarn and a magnificent, much-photographed view across to the Langdales.

> **Start/Finish**: National Trust pay and display car park at Blea Tarn
> (NY295043)
> **Distance**: 9km (5½ miles)
> **Height gain**: 315m (1,034ft)

1. Turn left out of the car park, cross the cattle grid and walk along the road for just over 1km.

> *This area is one of the last strongholds of the juniper bush. The Lake District used to be covered in huge forests of the stuff, but much of it has gone now. Its decline has been particularly marked over the last 50 years. Many old juniper bushes are not being naturally replaced owing to shading from other plants and grazing pressures from rabbits and livestock. Attempts are now being made in some parts of Cumbria to replant areas with young*

juniper bushes. In Longsleddale a few years ago, climbers were brought in to plant the conifers on inaccessible crags where they would be safe from sheep. The berries provide an important food source for birds and animals such as field mice, squirrels and badgers.

In the 17th century, the herbalist Nicholas Culpepper recommended the berries as a treatment for asthma and sciatica. He also claimed they could speed childbirth. If you get a chance, squeeze one of the berries and then sniff it. There's no mistaking which spirit this is used to flavour – gin.

2. Just before the road reaches the valley bottom, turn left up a grassy track with a low wooden barrier across it. You soon have a wall on your left as you make your way across some damp ground. As the wall starts to climb away from the path, you will see another one coming up from the right. This acts as your guide for the next 1.5km (1 mile). Just after a kissing-gate, ford a small beck. Turn right immediately after this, clambering over some rocks to gain a narrow, beckside route. As the beck quickly swings away, you rejoin the line of the wall. This pleasant path, which skirts the base of Lingmoor Fell, is a mostly good one, easy underfoot, but it does become a little rougher after passing the buildings at High Bield, where it briefly climbs more steeply. Keep to the path nearest the wall and you will eventually reach a gate.

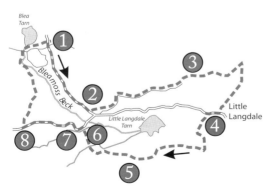

3. You will see a path heading

steeply up the fell to your left here, but you should go through the gate to continue in roughly the same direction. The clear path drops down through another couple of gates before reaching a wide track, along which you turn left. In 250 metres, go through the gate on your right – signposted Wilson Place. Ignore the track to the left early on. Swing left when you reach the farmyard and then turn right along the road.

4. Soon after passing the Three Shires Inn on your right, turn left along a surfaced lane – towards Tilberthwaite and Coniston. Cross the footbridge and then turn right along the rough, beckside track, passing the entrance to some disused quarries on your left in about 300 metres (see Walk 4).

5. Having passed two sets of buildings, you join a track coming down from the left and then bear right at a fork. After passing the pretty, white-washed cottage at Bridge End and crossing Greenburn Beck, the track makes directly for the Langdale Pikes in the distance.

6. Turn left when you reach the road, soon passing Fell Foot Farm. Just after the road swings sharp left, there is a gate on your left, which gives you access to a field next to the ancient ting mound behind the farm.

> *This is one of the few examples of ting mounds found in the UK. Norse settlers would have held important community meetings here – passing laws, trying criminals and making key decisions about the administration of the area. Ting mounds were normally located at convenient locations close to the centre of their area of influence. This one is in the centre of the Lake District fells and is close to the Roman road.*

7. Continue up the road, passing Castle Howe crag on your right. This road eventually leads up and over Wrynose Pass, but you leave it just 1km (¾ mile) after joining it.

The Romans built a road that went over the Wrynose and Hardknott passes, providing a link between the port of Glannaventa (now known as Ravenglass) and the fort at Galava (now Ambleside). Men and supplies from other parts of the empire would have landed at Glannaventa and then moved inland. From Galava, they could also have reached Brocavum (now Brougham, near Penrith) via High Street.

The Roman legions first entered the far north-west of England in about 71AD, when Petillius Cerialis began to crush the Brigantes, the Celtic people who dominated the region at the time. Agricola then managed to push north from Chester to Carlisle in 78AD and placed garrisons between the Solway Firth and the River Tyne. Although the Romans were soon clearly in charge and made allegiances with the Brigantes, the ancient Britons weren't truly quashed until about 140AD.

8. As soon as the wall on your left ends, turn sharp right (NNE) to strike off across a damp area. There is no path at first, but you soon pick up a clear route at the base of some steep ground. The path eventually passes alongside a pleasant, rocky gully. Go through a kissing-gate and bear right to cross a footbridge. This constructed path leads past Blea Tarn and comes out on to the road opposite the car park where the walk started.

The Three Shire Stone is located about 1.5km west of where the walk leaves the Wrynose Pass road. From at least 1671 the point at which the old counties of Cumberland, Westmorland and Lancashire met was marked by three small stones, inscribed with C, W and L respectively. (Cumbria as we know it today was set up during the local government reorganisation of 1974.) These had mysteriously disappeared by the beginning of the 20th century, but a limestone pillar, erected next to them in 1860 in memory of Cartmel's William Field, remained standing. This was damaged in the 1990s. It was subsequently repaired and three stones – copies of the original 'Three Shire Stones' – were also placed nearby.

RED SQUIRRELS

You might spot red squirrels on any one of the walks in this book, although they are becoming increasingly rare, even in Cumbria, one of their last strongholds. In most of the rest of England and Wales they have already been replaced by their grey cousins, introduced from North America in 1876. It is estimated that there are only a few thousand red squirrels left in the north of England. The greys out-compete the reds, particularly in lowland deciduous woodland, partly because the former breed more rapidly, with two litters a year, and partly because their extra body fat makes them better able to survive a severe winter. They have been known to displace the native species completely within seven years of arrival in a wood. Red squirrels are also more susceptible to certain diseases, particularly the devastating squirrelpox virus, and find it less easy to adapt when hedgerows and woodland are destroyed.

The Save Our Squirrels conservation project was set up in 2006 to try to protect reds in the north of England. Working with landowners in designated reserves, it helps develop and maintain habitat for red squirrels and eliminate any grey squirrels that enter the area.

8

Chapel Stile crags

Striding out above Langdale on an attractive, low-level ridge, walkers are treated to some lovely views of this famous Lakeland valley and its many popular crags and peaks. The climbs are short and well spaced-out, but the paths can be damp at times and there are one or two easy rocky sections to negotiate. There is also a slight risk of vertigo on a short section of path above Megs Gill.

> **Start/Finish**: National Trust pay and display car park in Elterwater (NY327047)
> **Distance**: 7km (4¼ miles)
> **Height gain**: 377m (1,235ft)

1. Leaving the car park via the vehicle entrance, turn right along the road and then, when it splits just after the Britannia Inn, bear left. Go straight across when you reach the main road through Langdale. Follow the minor road up towards the pretty white cottage of Braegarth and then round to the right, soon passing the recently renovated Wayside Pulpit on your left.

> *This was once a Pentecostal Mission Church, built in the 19th century when Elterwater was a thriving industrial settlement. Until recently, the one-storey chapel had been looking rather forlorn, after having been left to fall into disrepair in the mid-1990s, but it has now been refurbished.*

2. When the road swings left, leave it by turning right along a narrow path heading uphill beside a tiny beck. When this regains the road, cross diagonally to the left to gain a path, muddy in places, through

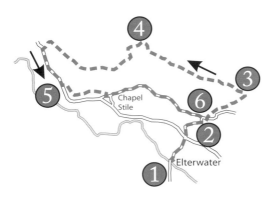

the bracken and grass. When you reach a fork near a squat stone structure housing an electricity sub-station, bear left up a steep, stony chute. As the path levels off slightly and you catch your first glimpse of the fells to the east, take the rocky path up the steep ground of Huntingstile Crag on your left.

The path at the base of Huntingstile Crag used to be a 'corpse road'. Until 1821, when a burial ground was consecrated at Chapel Stile, the people of Langdale were buried in Grasmere. Coffins had to be transported along this route to St Oswald's Church for interment.

3. You soon find yourself on a gorgeous, low-level ridge path undulating through bracken and rocky outcrops. There are lots of paths criss-crossing the fells in this area, but you want to head roughly NW for the next 1.2km, keeping reasonably close to the southern edge of the high ground. About 0.6km after gaining the ridge, clamber up to the cairn-topped summit of Dow Bank for a magnificent view of the Langdales. Continuing along the ridge from here, you cross a damp depression on stepping stones where you ignore the cairned path off to the left. Keep to the main path until you reach a large cairn at a junction of paths at the base of more rugged looking terrain.

4. Turn left here, heading steeply downhill on grass to pick up a narrow, rocky path that soon swings right, clinging to the side of the steep ravine. The path is very loose and there are steep drops to the left, so

watch your footing! After crossing a rocky area at the top of the Megs Gill waterfall, head steeply downhill with the gill to your left. When the stony path splits, bear right. At the next faint fork, keep right again to follow a pleasant, undulating path above Chapel Stile. Soon after passing a prominent crag to your left, the path begins descending. When the drystone wall on your left swings away, turn left to descend the steep, grassy slope alongside the wall. Head towards the small gate in a fence at the bottom of the slope and, once through, keep close to the wall on your right as you drop to the road. Turn left and walk along the asphalt for about 450 metres.

> *As you make your way along the road, you will see a group of huge boulders over the wall on your right. These erratics were deposited here by a glacier many thousands of years ago, and they form one of the most important prehistoric rock art sites in the north of England. Rediscovered in 1999, one of the boulders boasts a series of cup and ring markings believed to have been created between 3,000 and 5,000 years ago. They are difficult to make out, but what you are looking for are concentric circles, spirals and geometric designs arranged around a series of natural, circular depressions. There is an interpretation board, which helps a little.*

5. Eventually, you will see a signposted, grassy lane heading off to the left of the road. Take this. The path makes its way through some old quarry workings, never straying too far from the fence/wall on your right. It then emerges on the edge of Chapel Stile. When the lane splits in front of the church, keep left.

> *Fans of William Wordsworth's poetry may be interested to know that the churchyard here contains a gravestone with a long and poignant epitaph written by him in the 1840s. It marks the grave of the Rev Owen Lloyd (1803-1841) who was distantly related to Wordsworth and was a lifelong friend of Coleridge's eldest son, Hartley.*

Lloyd is credited with writing the hymn that is still sung at the rush-bearing ceremonies in Grasmere and Ambleside. This custom dates back to the time when church floors were made of mud and had to be strewn with rushes. Every year, the old rushes were removed and replaced with fresh ones. Of course, the earthen floors disappeared many decades ago, but the ceremonies live on in five Cumbrian villages – Ambleside, Grasmere, Urswick, Great Musgrave and Warcop.

6. Bear right at the next fork and then follow this road as it winds its way down to the main road through the valley. Cross straight over to retrace your steps to the car park.

WILLIAM WORDSWORTH

The name William Wordsworth is inextricably linked with Cumbria. He was born in Cockermouth on April 7, 1770, the son of a lawyer who worked as an agent for the wealthy Lowther family. He spent most of his childhood in Cockermouth and Penrith, his mother's home town. From 1779 until 1787, he attended Hawkshead Grammar School, and it was here that he was encouraged to write poetry.

After graduating from Cambridge, he travelled in Europe and spent some time living in Somerset with his sister Dorothy, but, with the 18th century drawing to a close, he returned to his beloved Lake District, setting up home in Grasmere and, later, Rydal. He married his childhood friend, Mary Hutchinson, in 1802, the couple eventually having five children.

The beauty of the landscape in which he lived, together with his love of walking, had a profound influence on Wordsworth's life and his poetry. Many of the 70,000 lines of verse that he wrote focus on the natural world.

9

BLACK FELL

Black Fell (323m) is a knobbly mass of bracken-covered hillocks and hummocks lying to the north of Tarn Hows. Standing isolated from the main fells with no other significantly high ground for two or three miles, its highest point, known as Black Crag, provides some surprisingly far-reaching views. As well as including a quick trot up to the summit, this route completes a circuit of the fell, so that you get to enjoy a range of landscapes. You'll be on good paths, tracks and quiet country roads for most of the time, but there is one short section that, in mist, could prove a little tricky from a navigational point of view.

Start/Finish: Roadside parking on the B5343,
near the Skelwith Bridge Hotel (NY344034)
Distance: 9.7km (6 miles)
Height gain: 382m (1,252ft)

---

1. From the junction of the B5343 Langdale road and the A593 in Skelwith Bridge, turn right, as if you are heading for Coniston. Cross the bridge over the River Brathay and follow the road round to the right. About 100 metres after passing and ignoring one footpath on your right, turn right along a track – signposted Elterwater and Coniston – and then quickly go through the gate on your left. After a second gate, keep left, parting company with the cycleway.

2. A little way beyond a third gate, join a rough track coming in from the left. After passing in front of Park House, head to the left of a tiny shed to pass through two metal kissing-gates in quick succession. The path leads up to Elterwater Park guesthouse. Swing left as you cross the yard to reach the access road. Cross diagonally to your right to pick

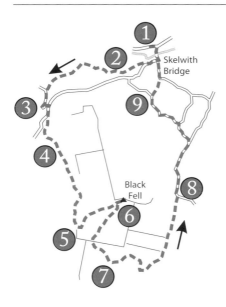

up the continuation of the footpath. The clear path crosses some stiles to reach another private road. Cross straight over and go through the gate to head downhill. After a couple more stiles and a short section of riverside walking, you reach a minor road along which you turn left.

3. At the next T-junction, turn right and walk along the main road for about 150 metres. Then, after passing a tiny layby on your left, cross over to head up some steps to a stile in a fence. Beyond this, follow the faint path away from the fence – to the right of a shallow ditch. Go through a gap in a wall and turn left along a rough track. This climbs gently to a gate in the wall on your left.

4. Beyond this, you find yourself on more open ground with the views becoming ever more impressive. Follow the line of the wall on your right for about 200 metres to reach a junction with a clearer track. Turn right here. Immediately after going through a gap in a wall near some old farm buildings, turn left along a slightly narrower path. This goes through one gate and then climbs to a second.

5. Immediately after this gate, turn left. The path is not obvious at this point, but you should keep close to the wall on your left for about 250 metres. You cross some boggy ground and then begin to climb. As the gradient levels off, bear right (NNE) along a faint path. This is very

indistinct as it winds its way across the open fell, but you will soon see the trig pillar on Black Crag about 400 metres to the NE – if in doubt, make directly for it; the route heads straight up the steep, western side of the fell, crossing a couple of tiny becks along the way.

As you reach the trig pillar, you'll be greeted by your first magnificent glimpse of Windermere. At nearly 17km long, Windermere is England's longest natural lake. It was created by the ice sheets of the last glacial period, which ended about 10,000 years ago. A glacier, which formed in the central part of the Lake District gouged out a deep, U-shaped valley as it ploughed southwards. This later filled with water to create the lake we see today.

The lake is home, all year round, to mute swans, moorhens, coots, mallard and mergansers. Grebes – little and great crested – tufted ducks and cormorants can also be seen. Wintering species include teal, goldeneye, goosanders and both Canada and greylag geese.

Beneath the water's surface, the famous Windermere char can be found. These fish, which grow to more than 3 metres in length, are said either to be relics of the last Ice Age or to have been introduced by the Romans. A deepwater trout, with delicate, pink flesh, it has always been regarded as something of a delicacy. Princes and politicians at the royal court would have tucked into it during medieval times, and char pies were once regarded as a very fashionable gift among the aristocracy. Today, potted char can occasionally be found on menus at local restaurants. The season runs from March to September when the fish are caught using two rods and shiny metal spinners.

6. Head SW away from the summit, on a clearer, cairned path. This eventually drops to a wide track near a wall. Turn left, through the

gate, and then take the next turning on your left – signposted Sunny Brow.

7. At a T-junction, turn left again, still following signs for Sunny Brow. The track winds its way down through an area of felled trees to a signpost at a wall. Turn left, towards Pullscar.

8. When you reach a minor road, turn left along it. Bear left at a fork – towards Skelwith and Ambleside. After passing some cottages at Bull Close, bear left at another fork – towards Coniston.

9. About 150 metres after passing a solitary dwelling on the left, turn right at a signpost to head downhill through the trees and alongside a fence on the right. Having crossed a beck, continue downhill to a rough track and then a minor road. Turn left here, and when you reach the junction with the A593, continue straight ahead, towards Ambleside. Now retrace your steps to the starting point.

> *The Talbot Bar in the Skelwith Bridge Hotel occupies the site of an old inn that is said to date back to 1600. It is named after the Talbot hounds, which were first introduced to England by William the Conqueror and the Talbot family, who came from Normandy and were later the Earls of Shrewsbury. The hounds died out in Europe in the 16th century, but continued to flourish in England and were sometimes used to guard the Scottish border. The breed finally died out in England at the beginning of the 19th century.*

10

LINGMOOR FELL AND SIDE PIKE

At 469m and 344m respectively, Lingmoor Fell and Side Pike are only small bumps on the Lakeland landscape, but don't be fooled into thinking you are in for an easy time – this is by far the most difficult route in this book, but all your efforts will be rewarded. With illustrious neighbours such as the Langdale Pikes, Wetherlam and Crinkle Crags towering over it, this has to be one of the best low-level fell walks in the whole of Cumbria – a sort of Lake District in miniature.

The walk on to Lingmoor Fell from Elterwater is fairly straightforward and mostly grassy on the top at first, but after that there are some exciting moments on the ridge with surprisingly steep sections of rocky descent and even a narrow rock squeeze that some people may find difficult. The return route then uses a pleasant, riverside path – a chance to relax after your earlier exertions.

> **Start/Finish**: National Trust pay and display car park
> in Elterwater (NY327047)
> **Distance**: 11km (6¾ miles)
> **Height gain**: 540m (1,770ft)

1. Turn left out of the car park and cross Great Langdale Beck. Walk along the road for about 300 metres and then, soon after passing the driveway of the Eltermere Inn on your left, turn right up a narrow lane – signposted Coniston. At a fork, bear right, soon passing a cottage called Ullet Nest on your right.

2. As you draw level with a solitary cottage in the woods on your right, turn left up a rough path – signposted Little Langdale. You quickly

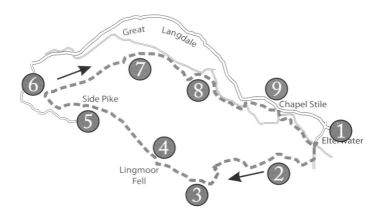

reach a junction with a wider forest track, along which you turn right. As you emerge from the trees near some disused quarry workings, the views of Langdale start to open up. Continue on the track for a further 500 metres beyond the wooden gate at the edge of the quarry. Don't be tempted by a path to the left heading up into the old workings; keep going until you see a small, white waymarker to the right of the track. This points you up a narrower, steeper path to the left. Follow this – it zigzags its way up to a gate in a wall. Cross the gate and continue uphill (S) for about 50 metres. Then turn right along the faint ridge path.

3. The path soon swings back towards the wall. There are several paths to choose from on the ridge; keep as close as possible to the wall. It's an undulating route and has a few twists and false summits along it, but the wall will eventually guide you to the cairn on Brown How, the highest point on Lingmoor Fell. You may lose sight of it on occasions. On one such occasion, you will crest a rise to get your first breathtaking view of Crinkle Crags and Bow Fell. From here, the ridge path drops and then climbs and then dips slightly again. The wall now swings sharp right and becomes a fence as it starts climbing more steeply. As it does so, the path briefly swings away from the wall. In

a few metres, bear right along a narrow, stony path climbing steeply. You soon regain the fence, which you will cross via a stile to reach the summit cairn.

4. Continue downhill with the dilapidated wall/fence on your immediate left. There is a long drop to Side Pike and the path is steep and rocky. When you reach a fence corner, turn left to descend steeply with the fence and then wall on your left. The wall continues to be your faithful companion guiding you down some rough ground. With the worst of the descent behind you, cross a stile and then continue downhill with the wall on your right. This path will take you all the way to the base of Side Pike's formidable buttresses straight ahead.

5. Cross a stile in a fence and then continue up towards the steep rock face. Only as you reach the base of the crag does the path finally swing left to find a route around the southern side of Side Pike. It clings tightly to a ledge and then squeezes its way through a narrow gap between the rocks. The path soon swings right and climbs. When the Langdales reappear, the path splits. Bear right if you want to climb to the summit of Side Pike, but the main route goes left. Follow the wall on your right until the path goes through a gap in it. With the ground suddenly dropping away steeply, the route ahead is unclear. Basically, you need to pick up a path, cairned in places, that negotiates several shallow rocky ledges to descend in a mostly WSW direction. When you reach the drystone wall at the base of the fell, turn right.

6. The path eventually drops to some woodland. Don't go through the gate at the edge of the trees; instead turn right to walk with the fence on your left. The faint path goes through a kissing-gate and becomes even fainter (and wetter underfoot) when you leave the area of woodland on your left behind. Make sure you continue walking parallel with the wall about 200 metres up to your right. Eventually, the route becomes a little clearer and crosses a ladder stile. After a second stile and bridge above Side House, bear left to walk beside a tiny beck. Don't cross the bridge near the buildings; instead turn right along the clear path.

7. After the next kissing-gate, the path climbs, but then drops back to the valley bottom again. When you reach a fingerpost near an old stone barn, keep straight ahead – signposted Great Langdale Road. The path quickly swings left to pass in front of a cottage called Oak Howe.

> *The cottage you see here today is not the original one; the first Oak Howe was burned down by local people in the 17th century. Legend has it that the family living there had a son who was away in London during the 1660s. He died of the plague and his clothes were returned to the family home in Langdale. Unfortunately, the clothes were carrying the disease and his entire family succumbed. They all died and were buried in the garden, a laurel tree being planted over each of their graves.*

8. Don't be tempted by the bridge over Great Langdale Beck in a short while; just keep following the clear, wide track downstream. It eventually crosses a humpback bridge and then swings right. When it then swings left near the road, leave it by turning right along a path. As you reach the buildings, follow the sealed road to the left. Then, making sure you don't head up to the farm buildings, turn right at the next track junction to walk with the school's wall on your left. Keep the wall on your left until you drop to the road.

9. Turn right and, soon after passing the Wainwright's Inn, turn right again to cross Great Langdale Beck via a footbridge. Once on the other side, turn left. Eventually, you reach a minor road along which you bear left. Turn left at the T-junction to return to the car park.

> *Elterwater has a strong link with the German 'Merzbau' art movement. This was invented and developed by the Hanover-born artist Kurt Schwitters who was forced to flee Germany in 1938 after he discovered that he was wanted for 'interview' by the Gestapo. Travelling via Norway and then Scotland, he reached England and*

eventually settled in Ambleside.

He used an empty barn on the site of the former gunpowder works at Elterwater as a studio – or, more precisely, as a medium for his work. Over a period of 18 months, he sculpted its interior by creating shapes out of plaster and embedding items into its walls. Sadly, the work remained unfinished and Schwitters died in poverty in 1948. Seventeen years later, however, the barn wall was dismantled and carefully transported to Newcastle University. It is now on display at the city's Hatton Gallery.

In early 2011, Cumbrian drystone wallers created a replica of Schwitters' barn in the courtyard of the Royal Academy of Arts in London. It formed part of the Modern British Sculpture exhibition, standing alongside work by Barbara Hepworth, Henry Moore and Damien Hirst. Other smaller sculptures Schwitters made in the barn are now on display at London's Tate Modern gallery.

There are plans to restore the original Elterwater barn and build a small museum nearby. Amid growing recognition of Schwitters' influence on modern art – particularly the pop art movement – the Manchester-based charity Littoral bought the site in 2006 and, at the time of writing, was busy raising money for the restoration project.

Other titles by
QUESTA PUBLISHING LIMITED

LAKE DISTRICT
WALKS WITH CHILDREN
Buttermere and the Vale of Lorton
Around Coniston
Keswick and the Newlands Valley
Ambleside and Grasmere
Ullswater
Around Kendal
Around Windermere
South Lakeland

EASY RAMBLES
Around Keswick and Borrowdale
Around Ambleside and Grasmere
Around Eskdale
Around Wasdale
Around Ennerdale & Calder Valley
Around Dunnerdale
Around Coniston and Hawkshead
Around Patterdale and Ullswater

YORKSHIRE DALES
WALKS WITH CHILDREN
Wharfedale
Swaledale
Wensleydale
Malham and Airedale
Ribblesdale

PEAK DISTRICT
WALKS WITH CHILDREN
Dark Peak

PENNINES
SHORT WALKS
Eden Valley and North Pennines

All QUESTA titles are available from
27 Camwood, BAMBER BRIDGE, Lancashire PR5 8LA
or by FAX to
0705 349 1743

www.questapublishing.co.uk